Copy. Print. Trace. Learn. Repeat.

ABCDEFGHIJKLM
NOPQRSTUVWXYZ

ABCDEFGHIJKLM
NOPQRSTUVWXYZ

ABCDEFGHIJKLM
NOPQRSTUVWXYZ

ABCDEFGHIJKLM
NOPQRSTUVWXYZ

Copyright

Alphabet Jam
UPPER CASE LETTERS & lowercase letters

Written and illustrated by Tina Cambio
Digitally printed.

ISBN Hardcover: #978-0-9896028-4-6
ISBN Paperback: #978-0-9896028-9-1
Library of Congress Control Number: 2015909372

Ⓒ 2015 Tina Cambio

All rights reserved. No part of this publication may be reproduced, distributed, or transmitted in any form or by any means, including photocopying, recording, or other electronic or mechanical methods, without the prior written permission of the publisher except for the "copy, print, trace, learn and repeat" end sheets, which may be used for noncommercial, nonprofit, educational purposes only.

Published by

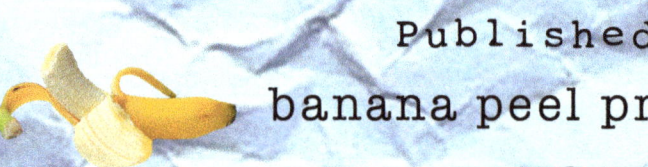

banana peel press, LLC

USA

Contact us at
www.bananapeelpress.com
for current wholesale information
and other questions.

Avocado

Fresh. Ripe. Mushy. Yummy.

Butterfly

Gentle. Flap.
Flutter. Fly.

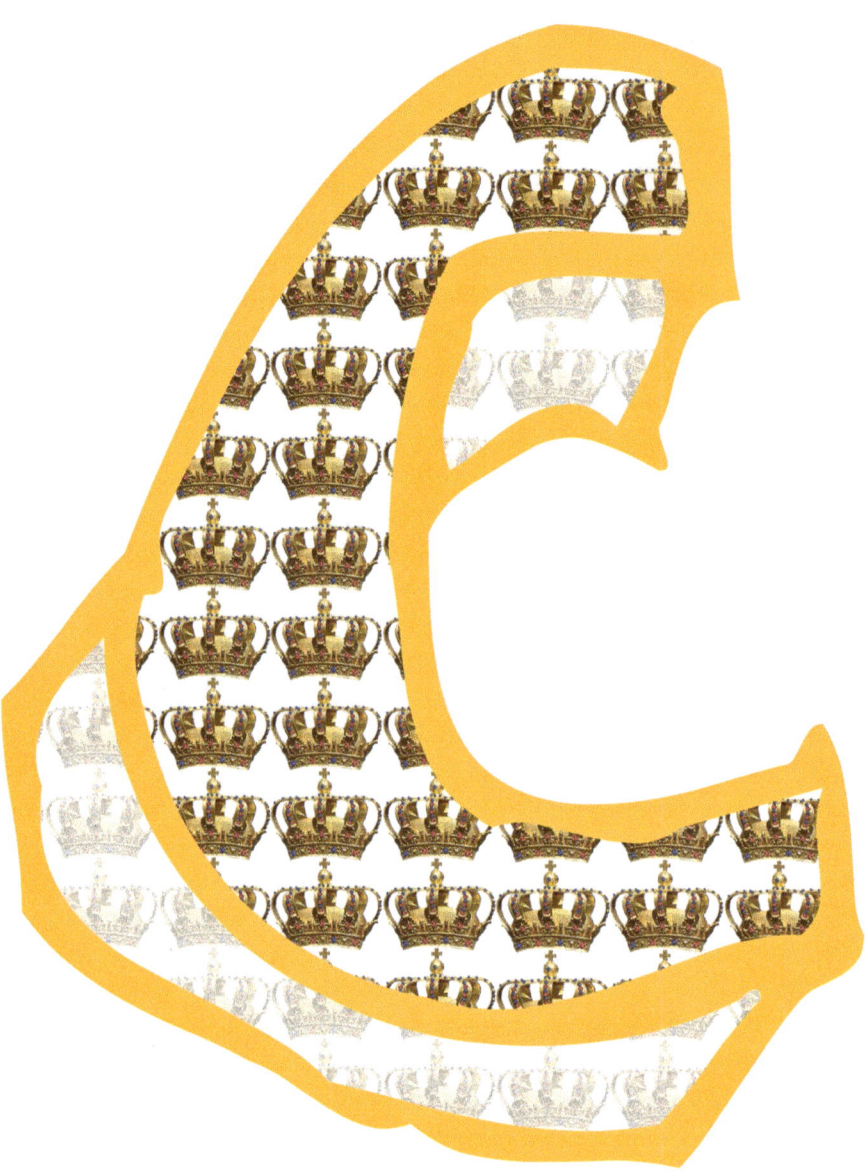

Crown

Royal. Jewels.
King. Queen.

Daisy

Grow. Petals. Stem. Sniff.

Egg

Toast. Dunk.
Drip. Eat.

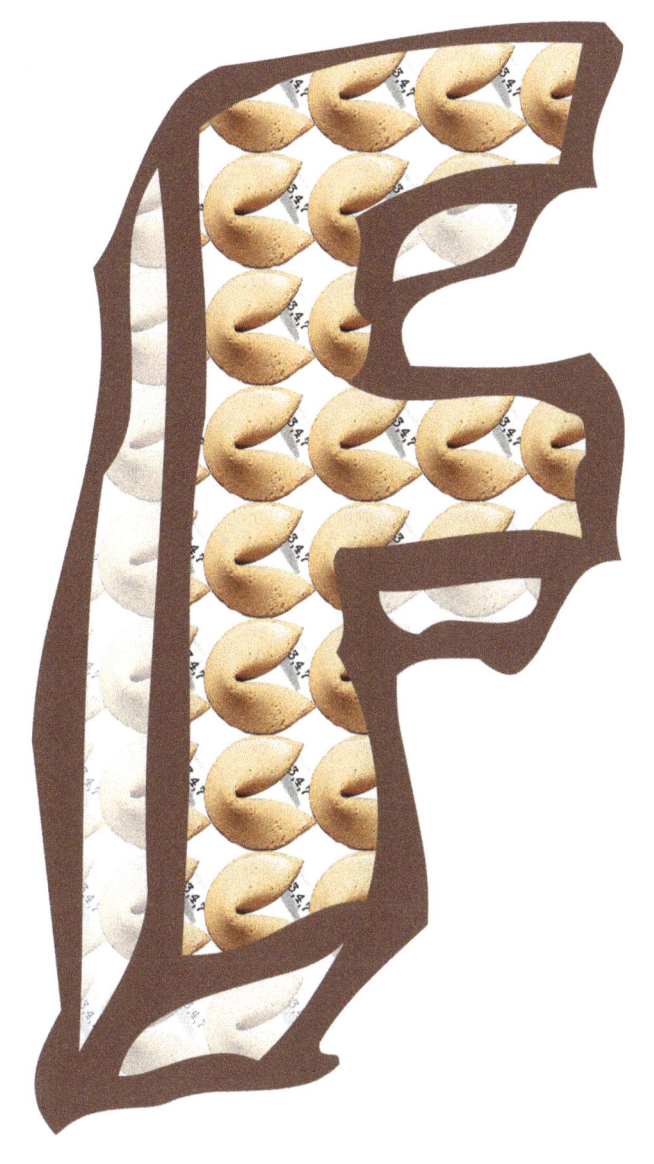

Fortune cookie

Break. Read.
Lucky. Loved. Happy.

Grasshopper

Insect. Musical. Hoppy. Summer. Loud.

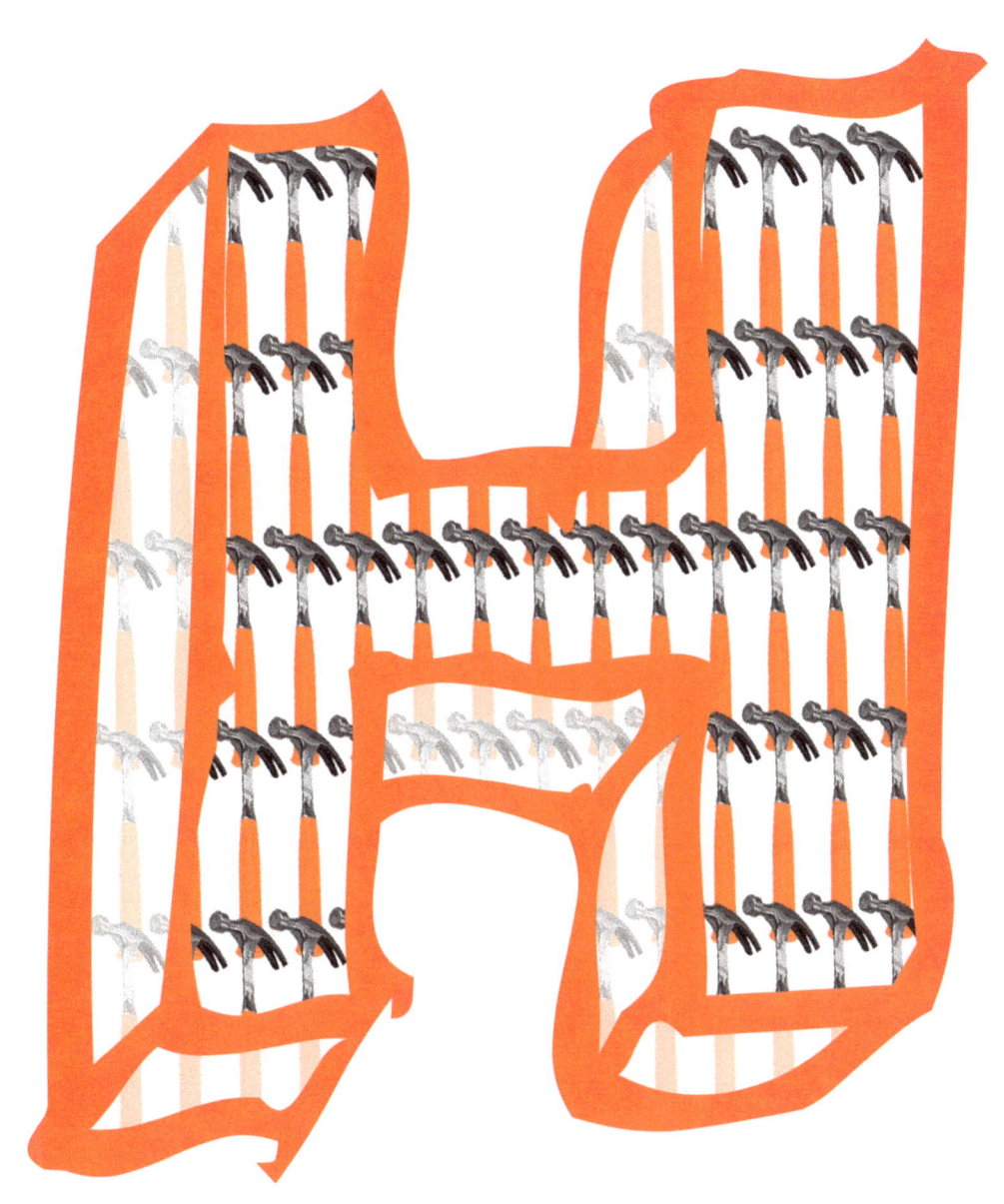

Hammer

Heavy. Tool.
Pound. Nail.

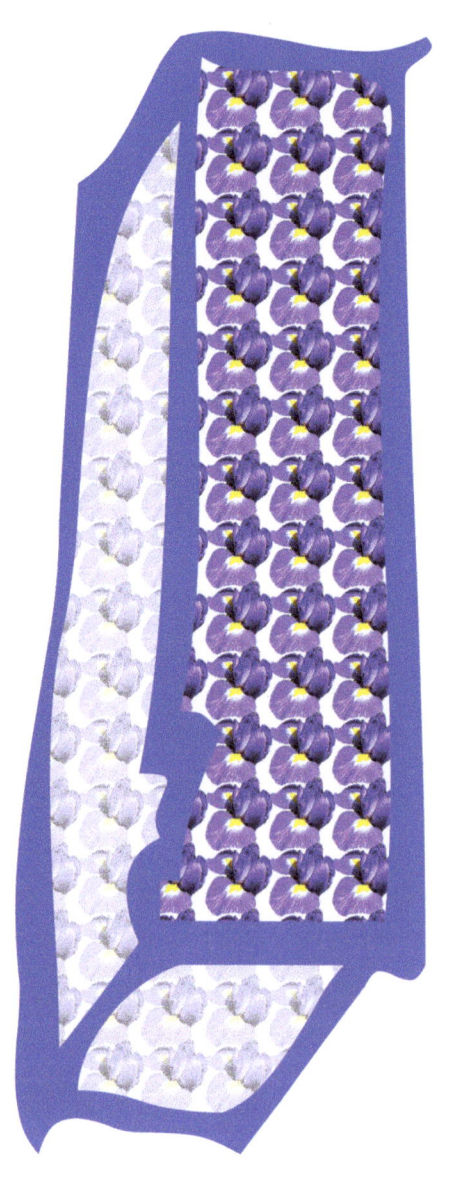

Iris

Flower. Plant.
Bloom. Colorful.

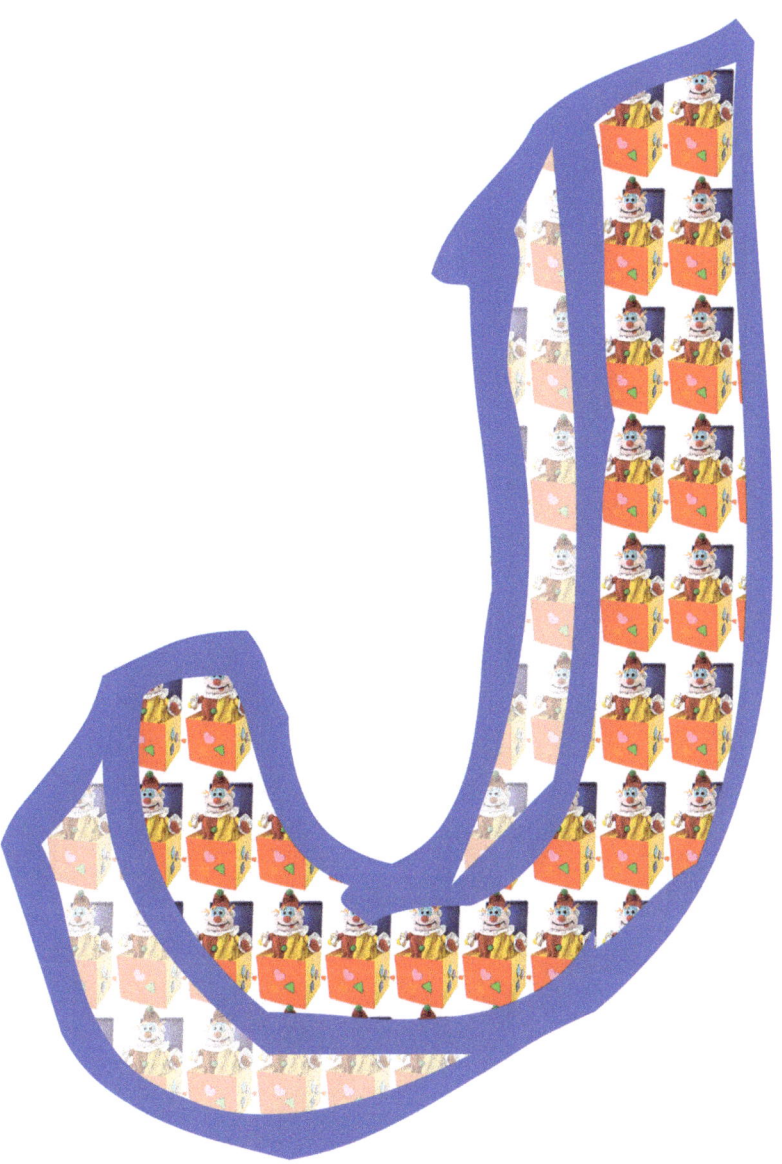

Jack In The Box

Toy. Crank.
Wait. Peek a boo!

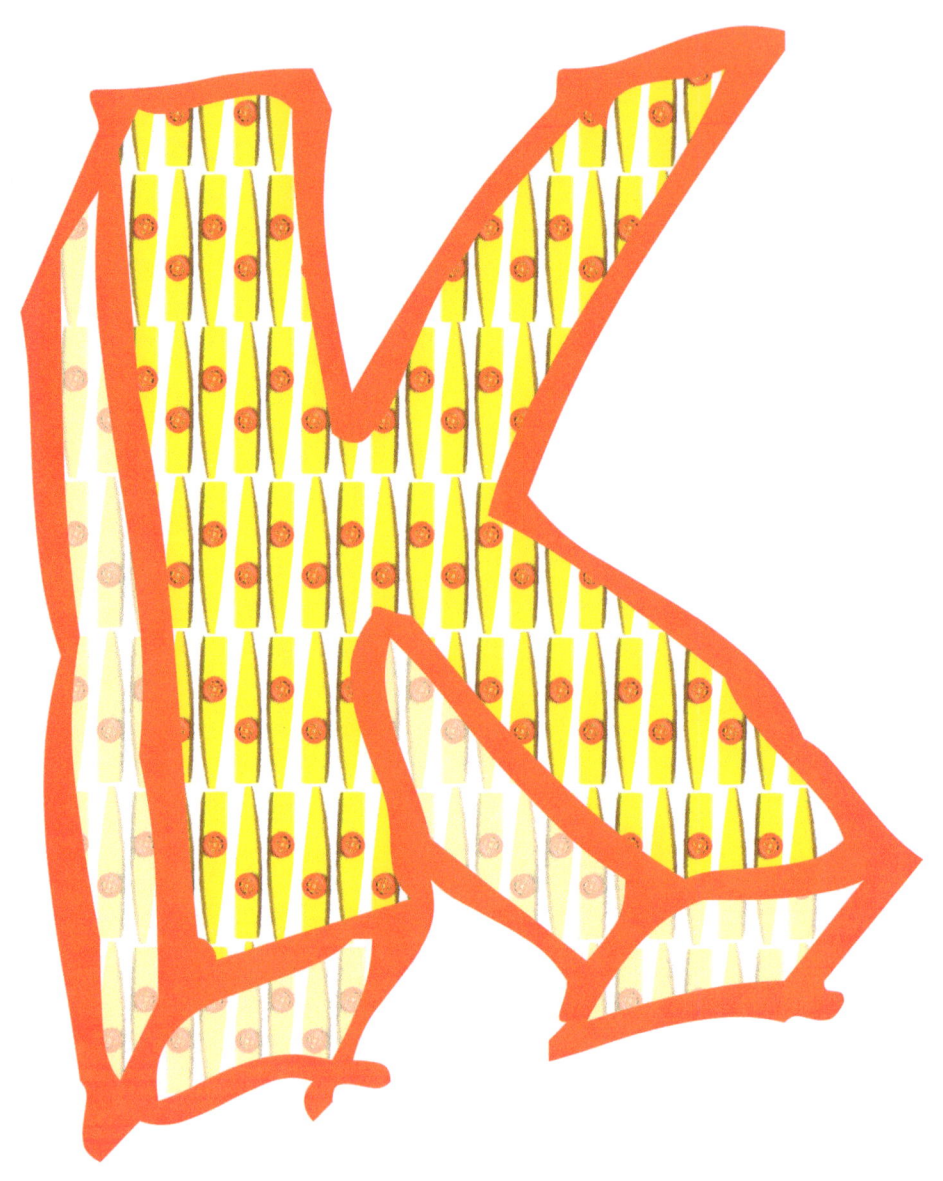

Kazoo

Tube. Hole. Blow.
Buzz. Buzz. Buzz.

Lion

King. Jungle. Strong. Fast. Roar.

Mug

Empty. Full.
Hot. Cold.

Nuts

Crack. Chomp.
Roasted. Salty.

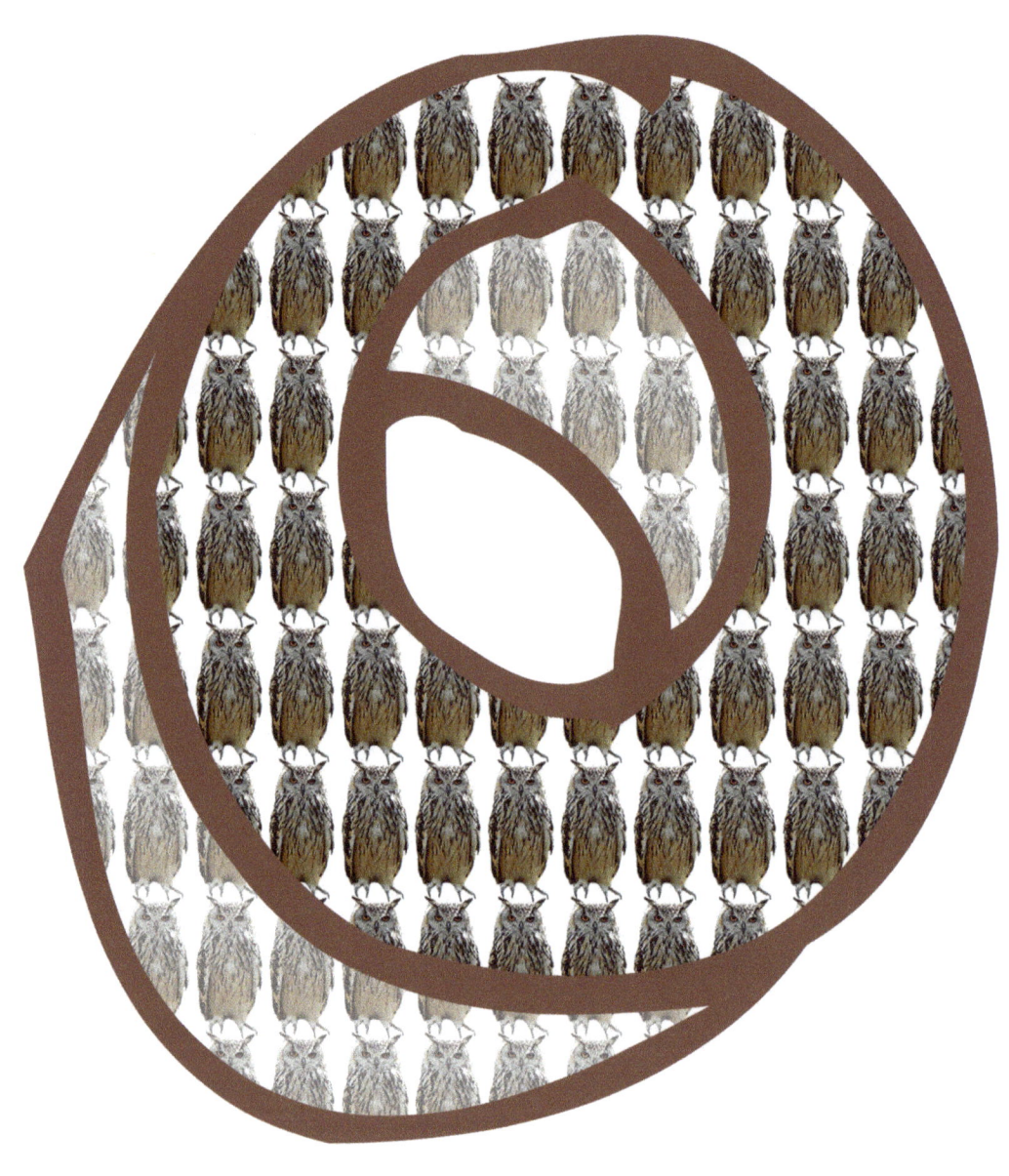

Owl

Wild. Brown. Spotted.
Hoo. Hoo. Hoo.

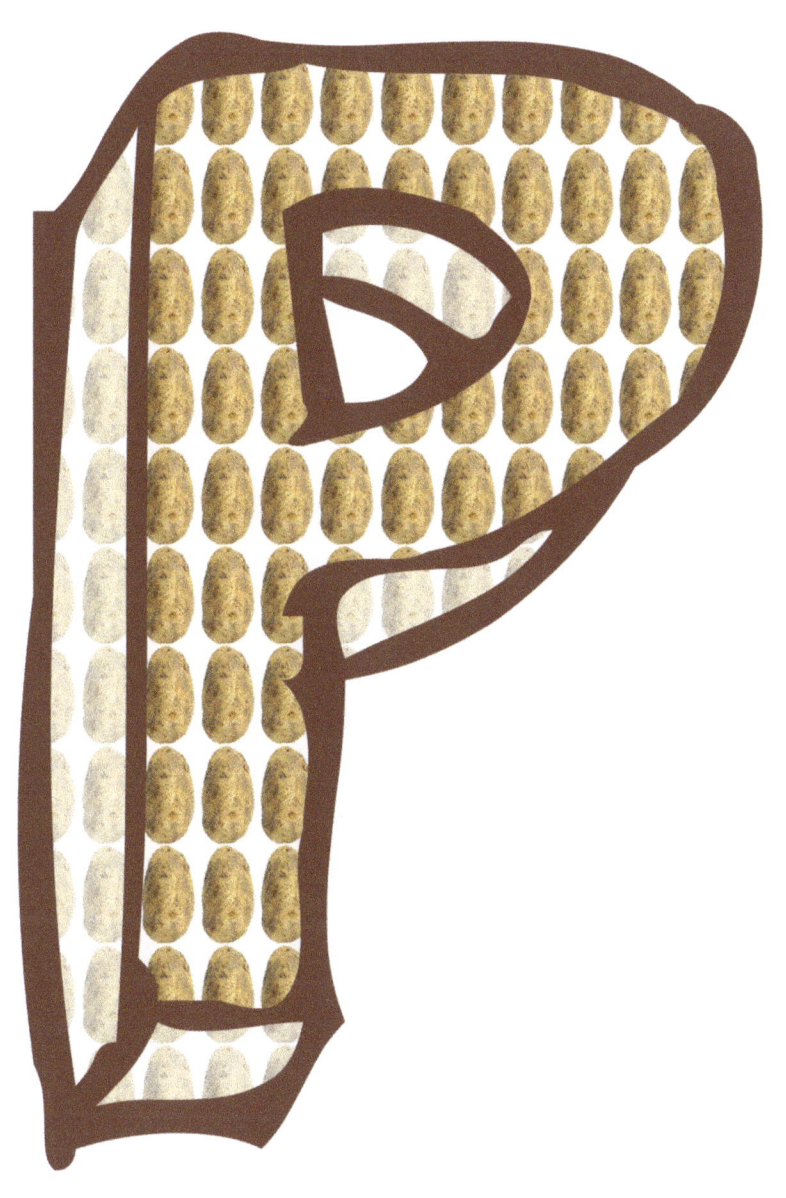

Potato

Chips. Baked.
Fried. Mashed.

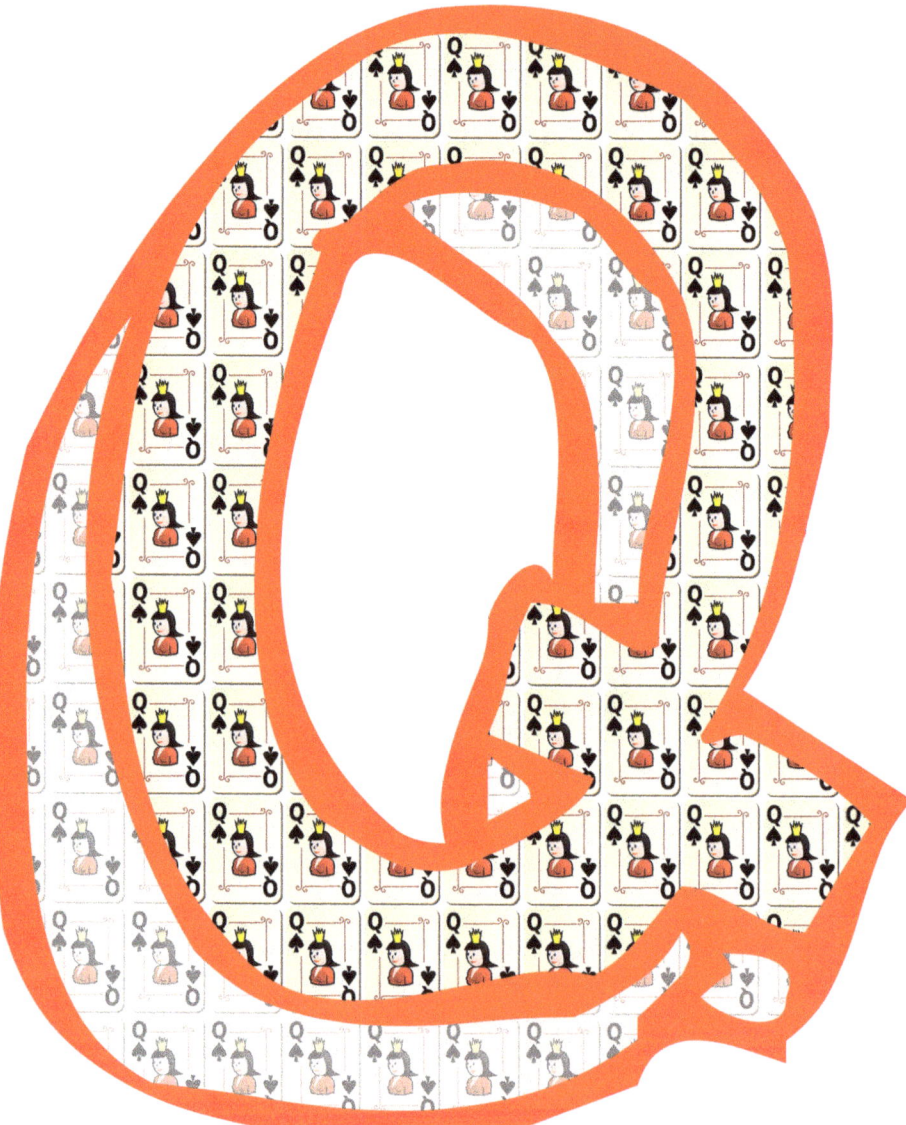

Queen

Play. Card.
Spades. Game.

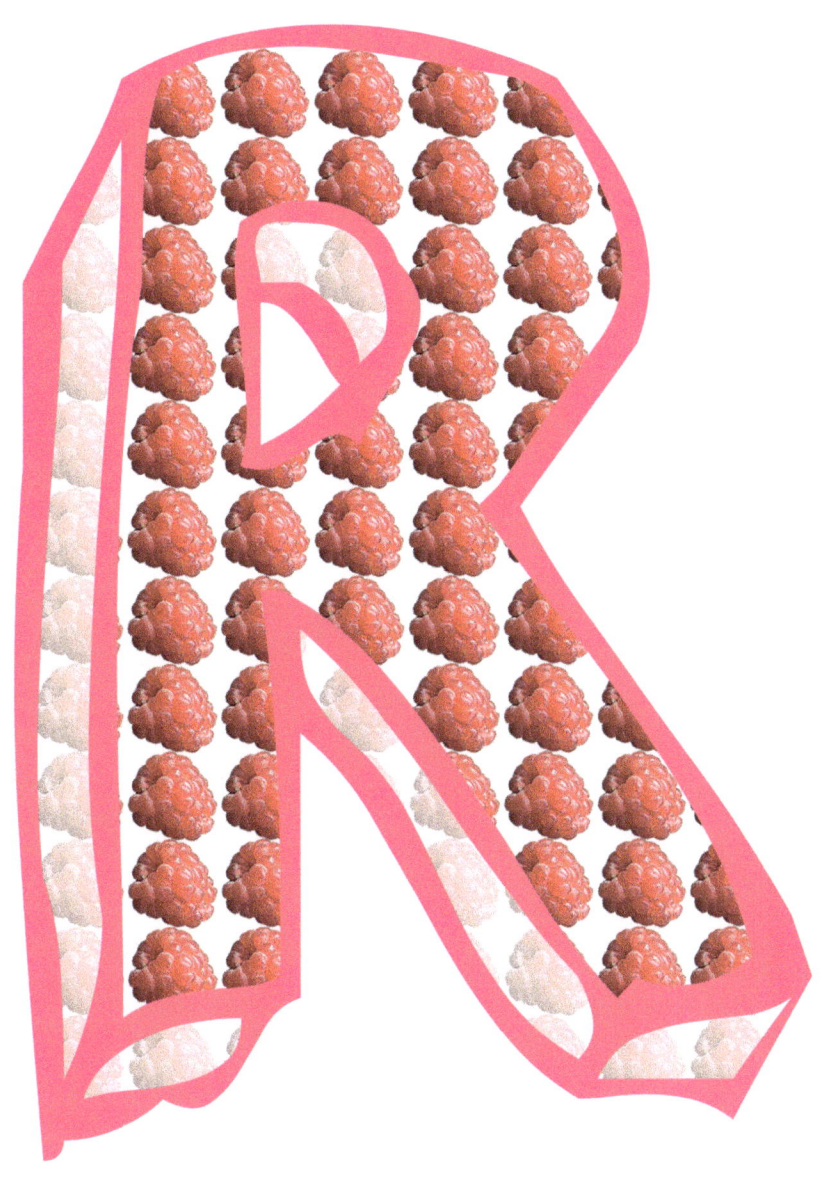

Raspberry

Bumpy. Squishy.
Tart. Fuzzy.

Sandwich

Bread. Crust.
Peanut butter. Jelly.

Taco

Shell. Meat. Tomato. Lettuce. Onion. Cheese.

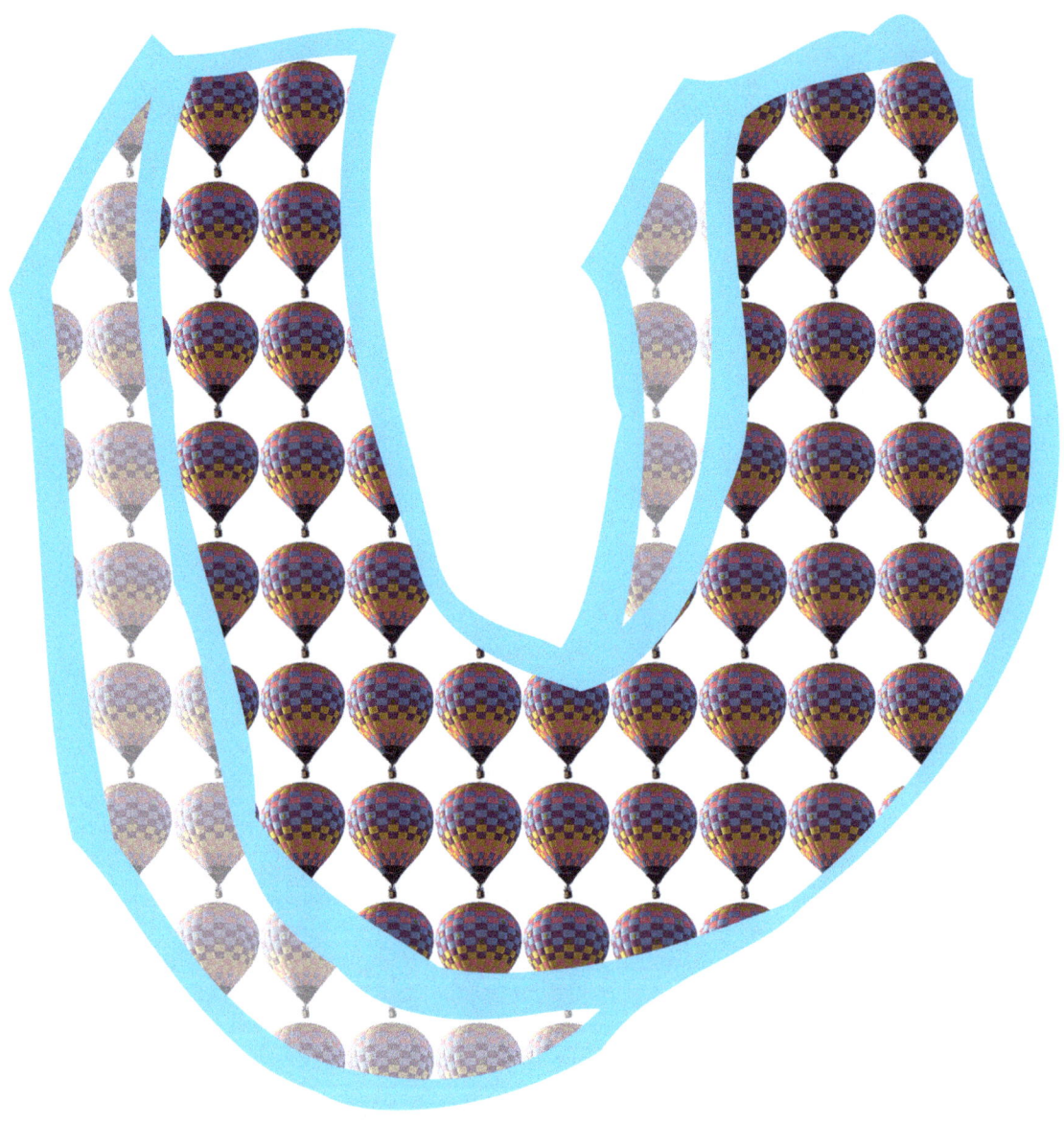

Up

Sky. High.
Balloon. Above.

Valentine

Holiday. Love.
Kiss. Hug.

Watch

Wear. Wrist. Time. Tick. Tock.

X ray

Machine. Scan.
Waves. Image.

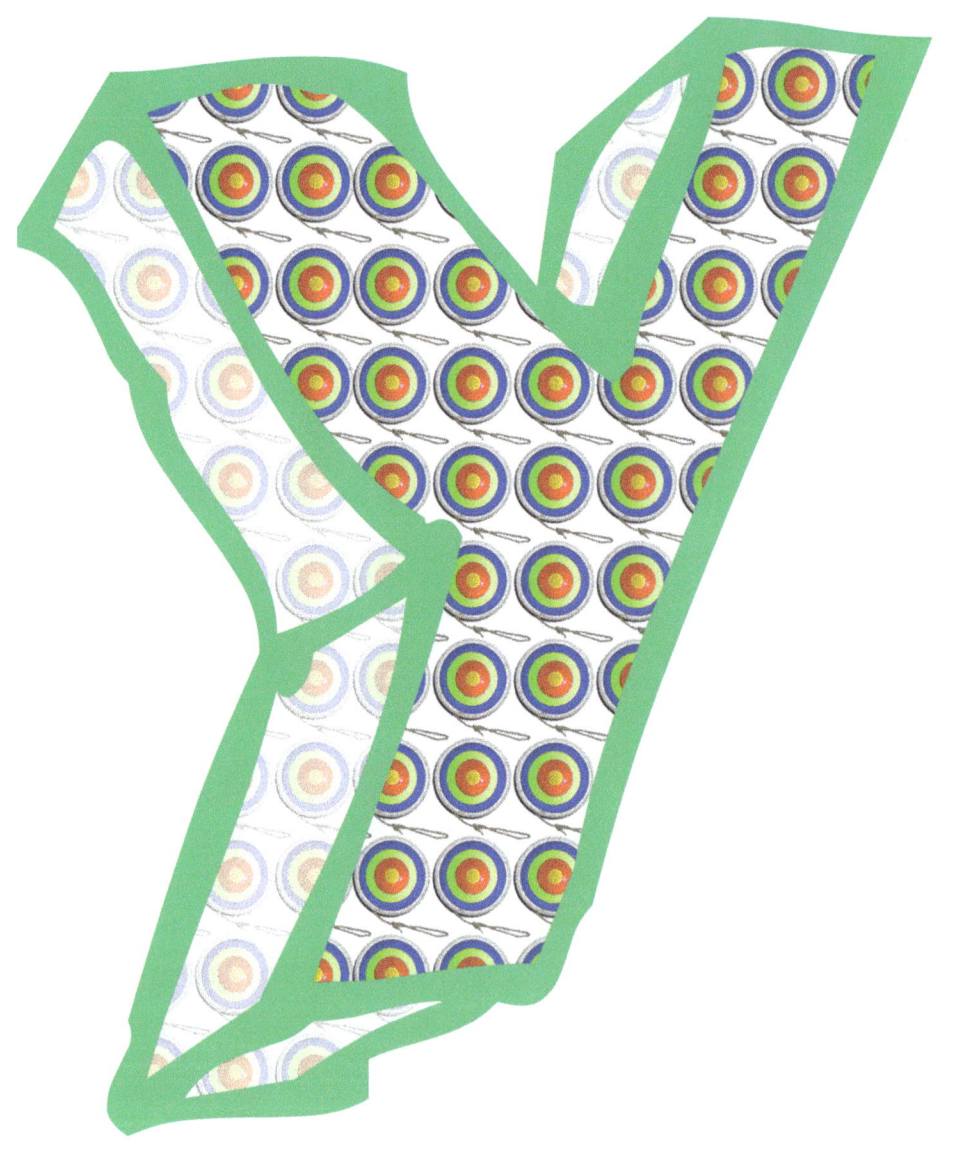

Yo yo

Up. Down.
String. Tricks.

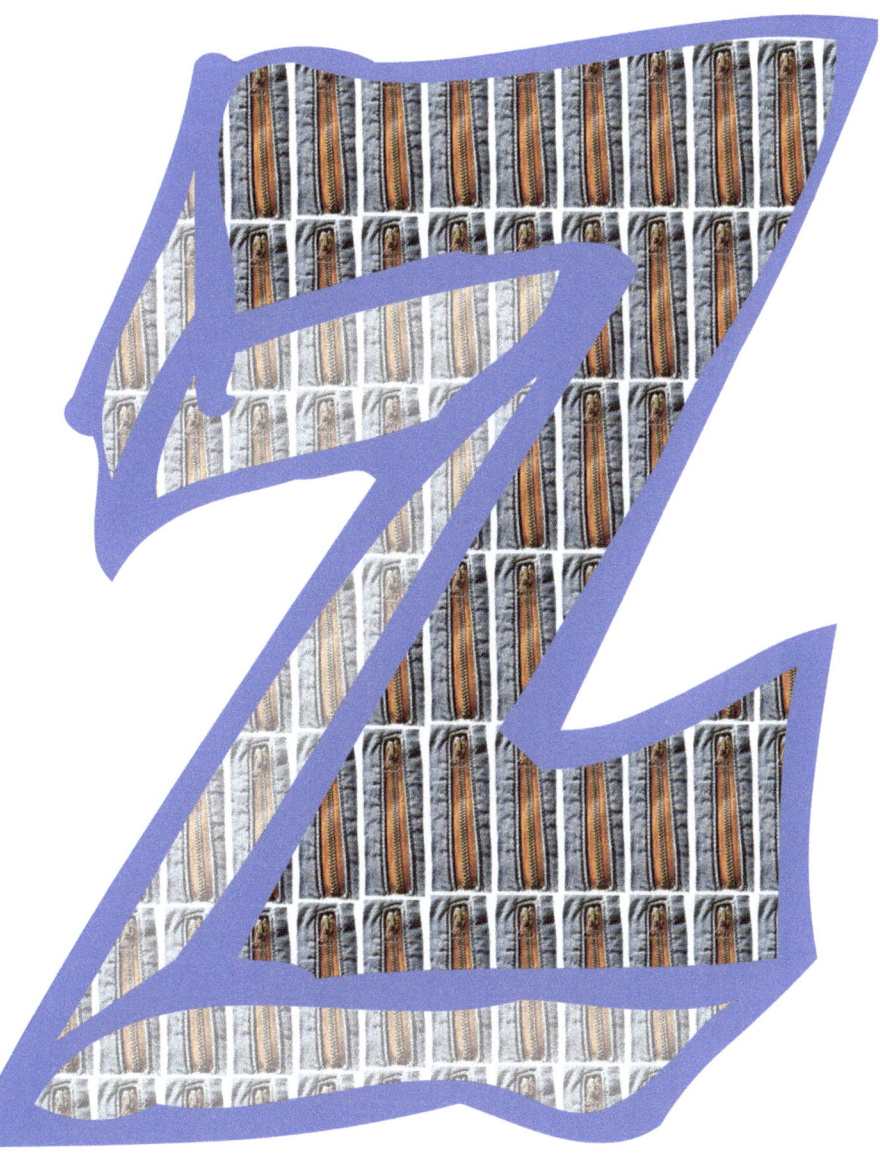

Zipper

Teeth. Slider.
Fly. Tracks.

Copy. Print. Trace. Learn. Repeat.

Avocado Butterfly
Crown Daisy Egg
Fortune Cookie
Grasshopper
Hammer Iris
Jack In The Box
Kazoo Lion Mug
Nuts Owl Potato
Queen Raspberry
Sandwich Taco Up
Valentine Watch
X ray Yo yo Zipper

Copy. Print. Trace. Learn. Repeat.

apple bicycle

cupcake duck

envelope fish

gumball harp

ice cream

jellybeans key

lemon music noodle

olive puzzle quarter

rock starfish tea

umbrella violin whale

x marks the spot

yarn zebra

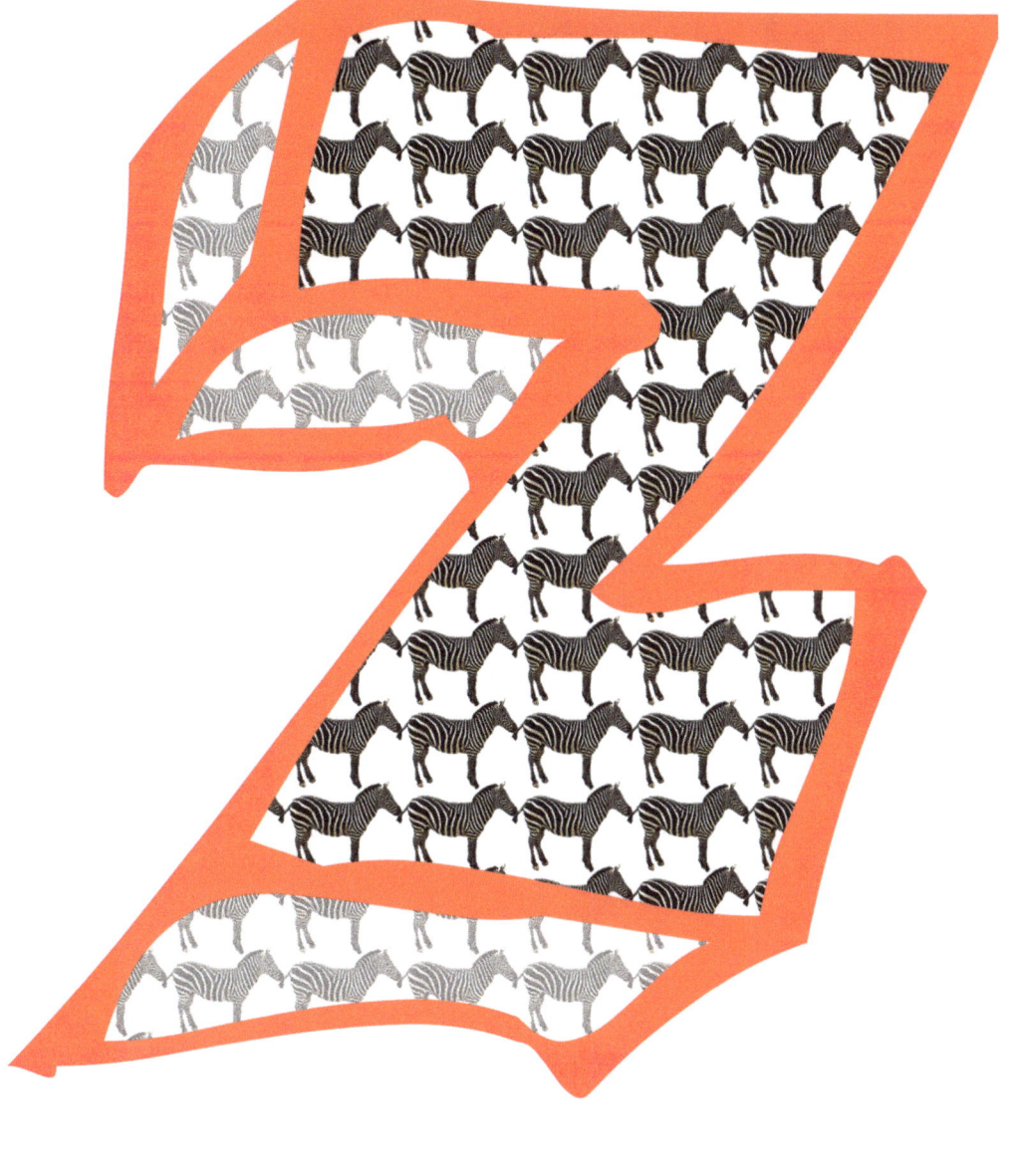

zebra

Striped. Pattern.
African. Horse.

Yarn

Fiber. Ball.
Knit. Weave.

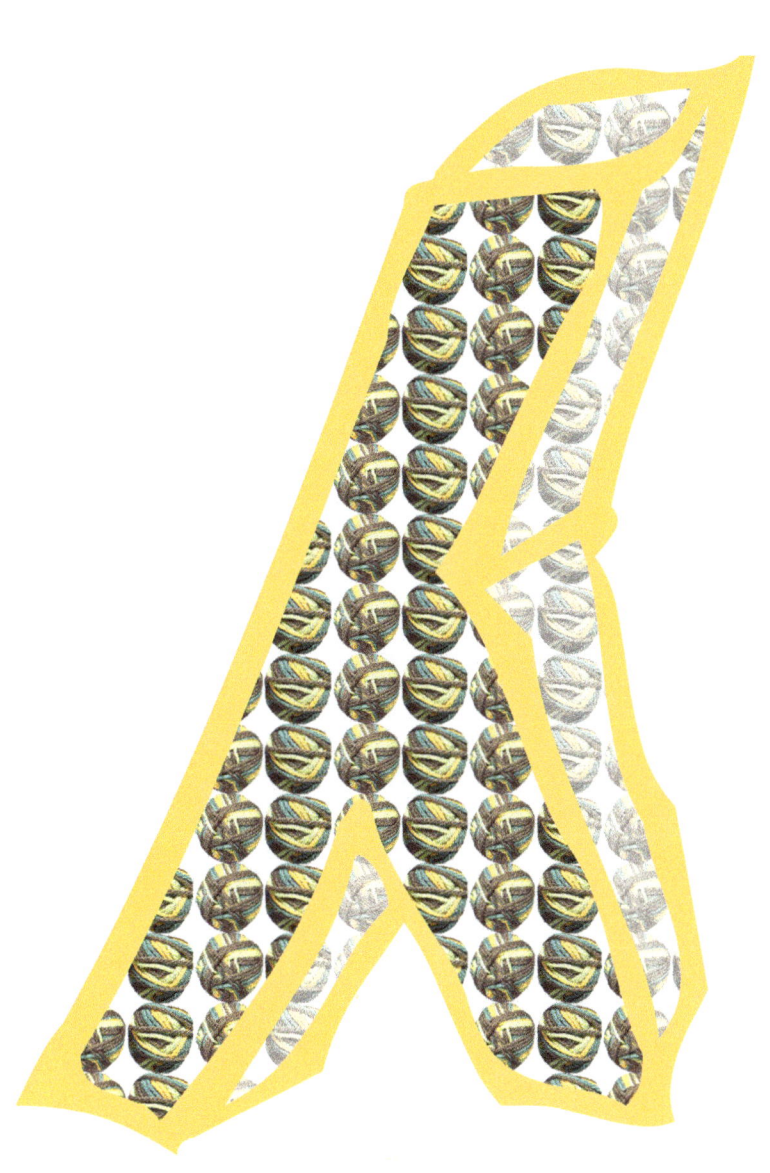

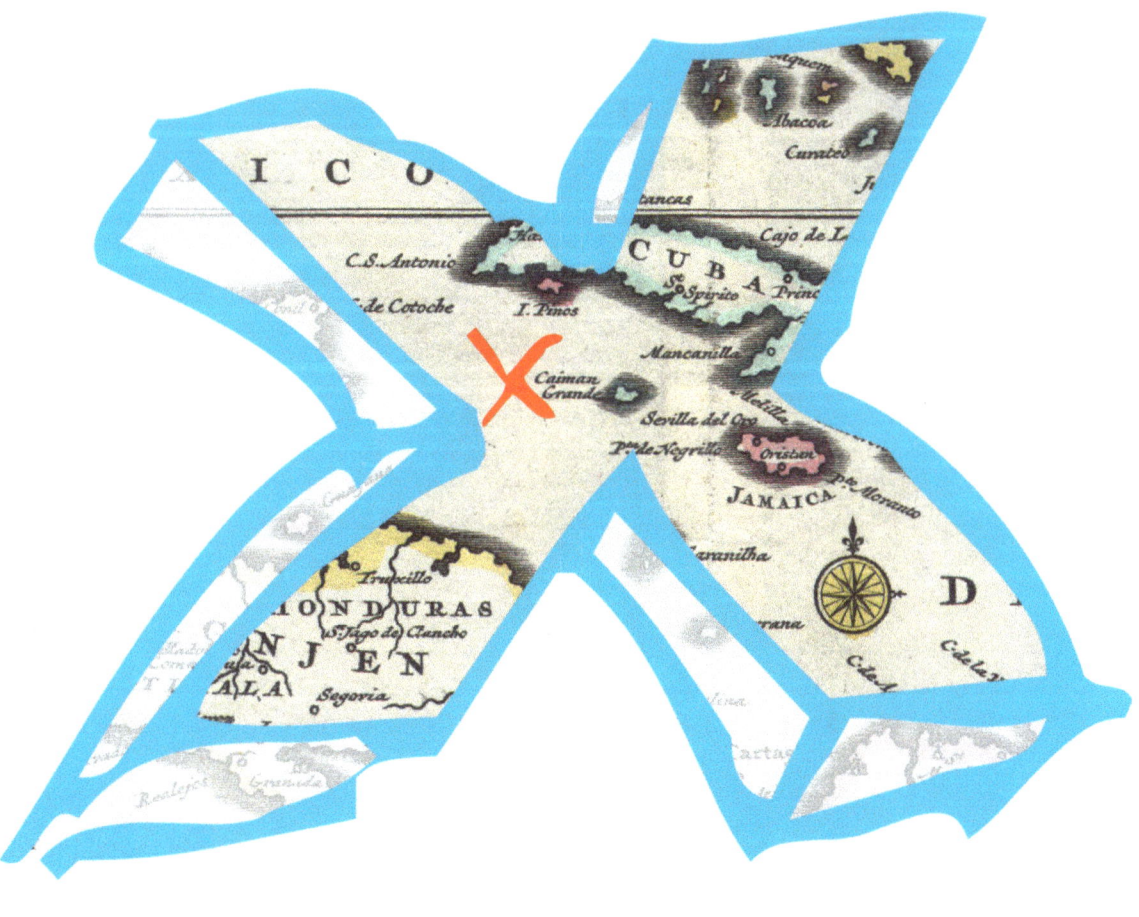

x marks the spot

Map. Compass.
Location. Treasure.

Whale

Mighty. Huge.
Black. White.

violin

Instrument. Mellow. Strings. Bow.

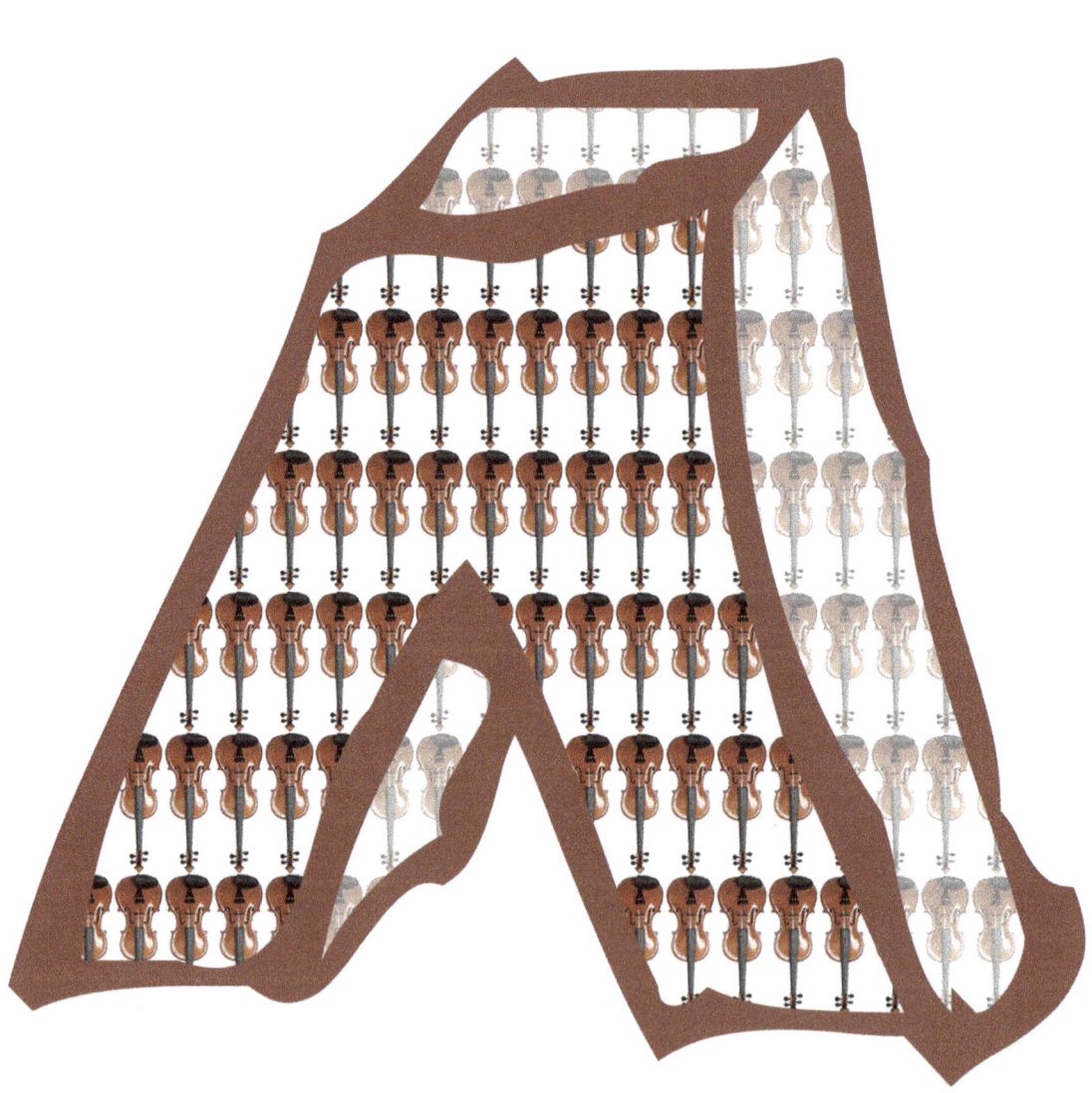

umbrella

Rain. Wet.
Open. Cover.

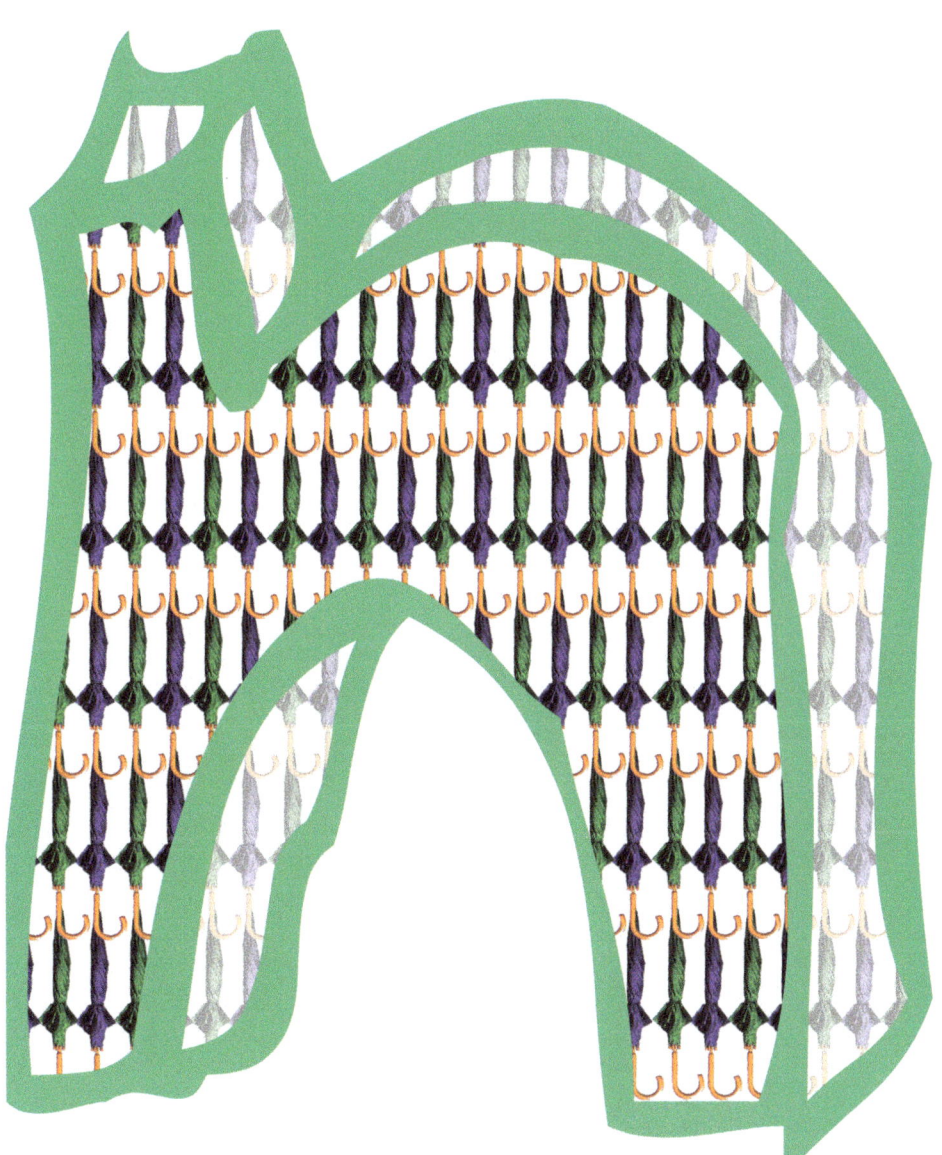

tea

Loose. Leaf.
Dry. Bag.

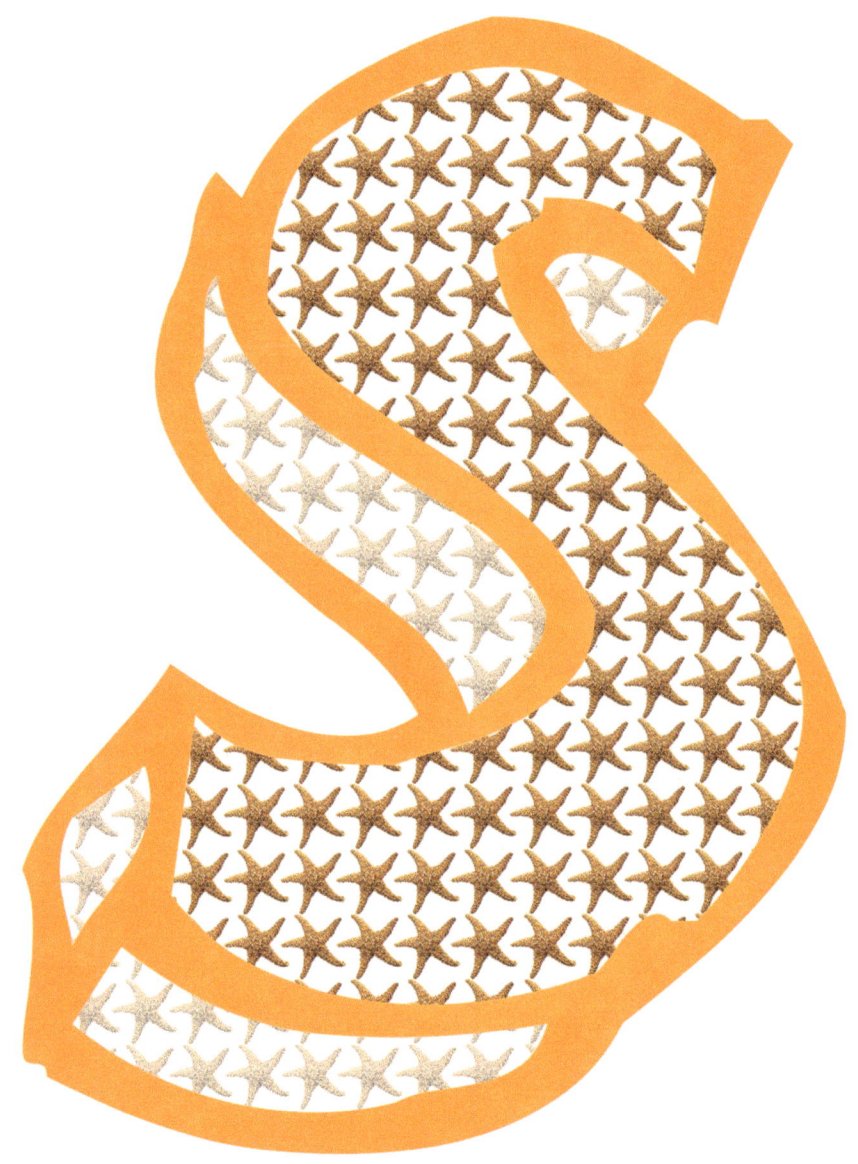

starfish

Ocean. Water.
Tube feet. Arms.

rock

Stone. Hard.
Solid. Pebble.

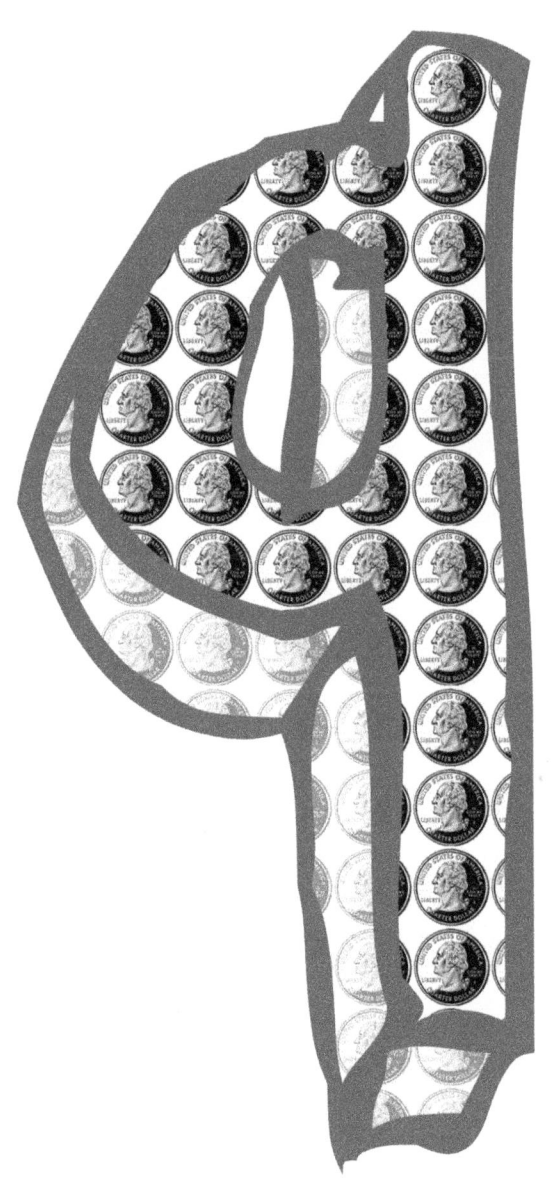

quarter

Coin. Money.
Heads. Tails.

puzzle

Piece. Edge. Connect. Picture.

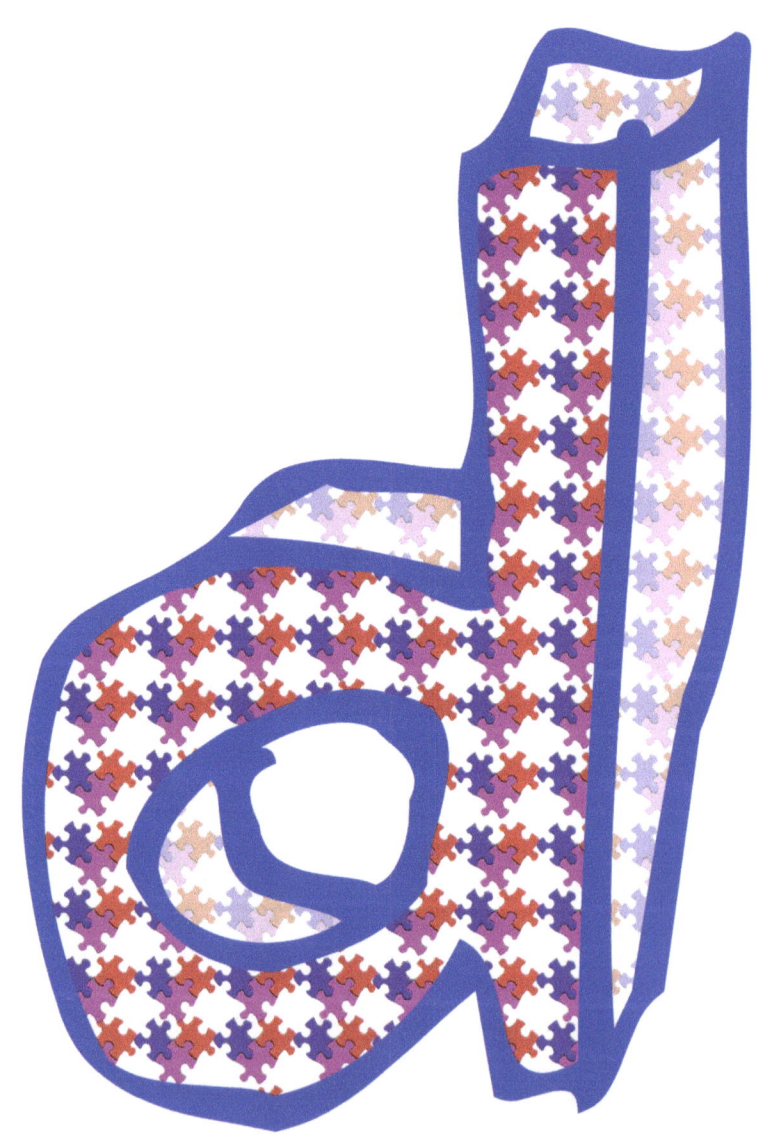

Olive

Bitter. Smooth. Oval. Pit.

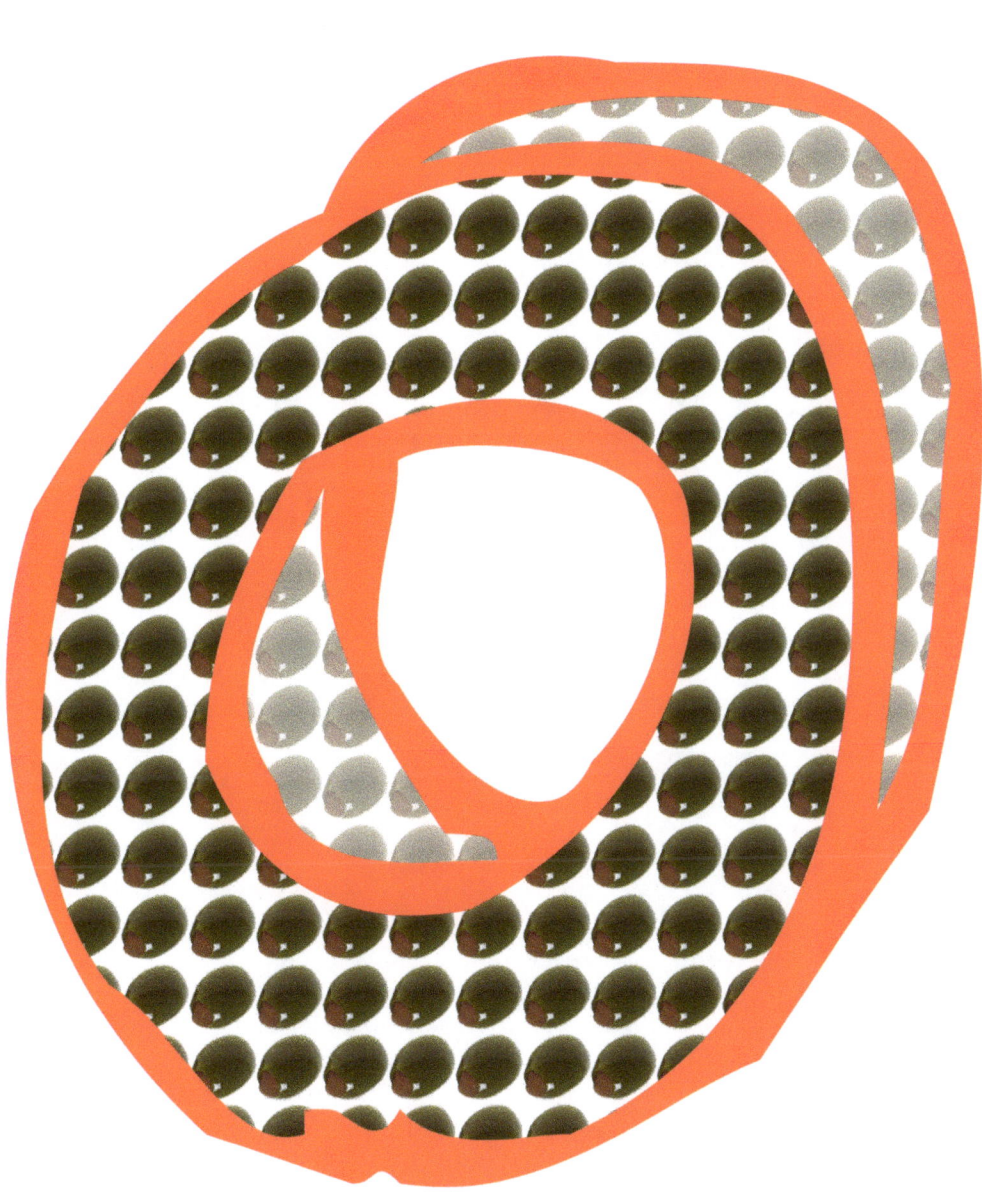

noodle

Twirl. Slurp. Chew. Swallow.

music

Notes. Voice. Sounds.
Fa. La. La.

Lemon

Citrus. Juicy.
Sour. Pucker.

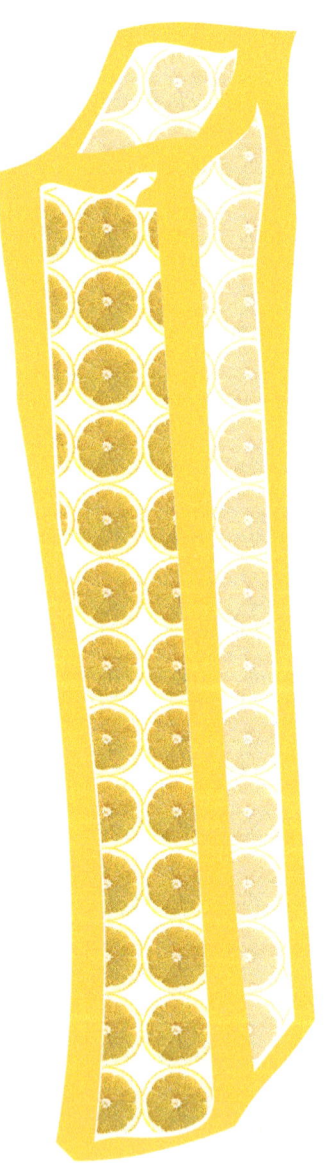

key

Close. Click. Lock.
Click. Unlock. Open.

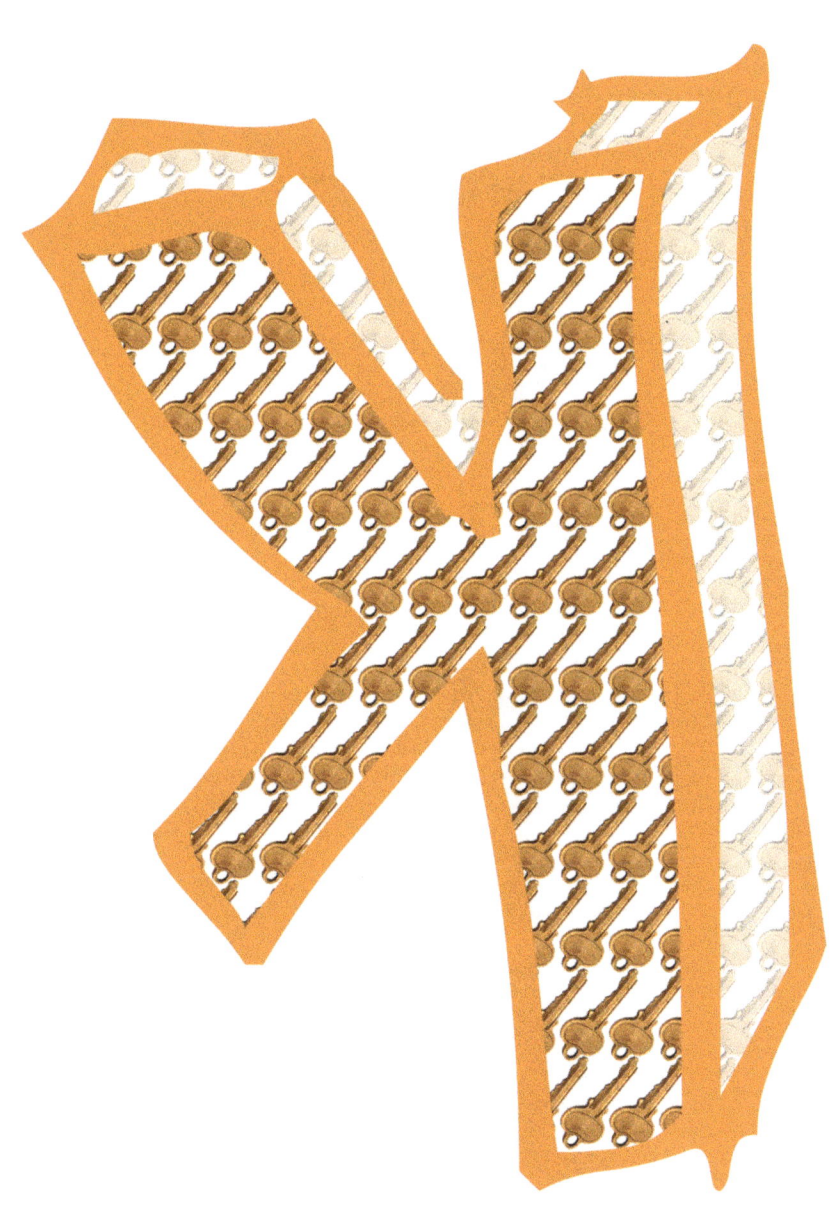

jellybeans

Fruity. Gooey.
Sugar. Candy.

ice cream

Cold. Frozen.
Creamy. Treat.

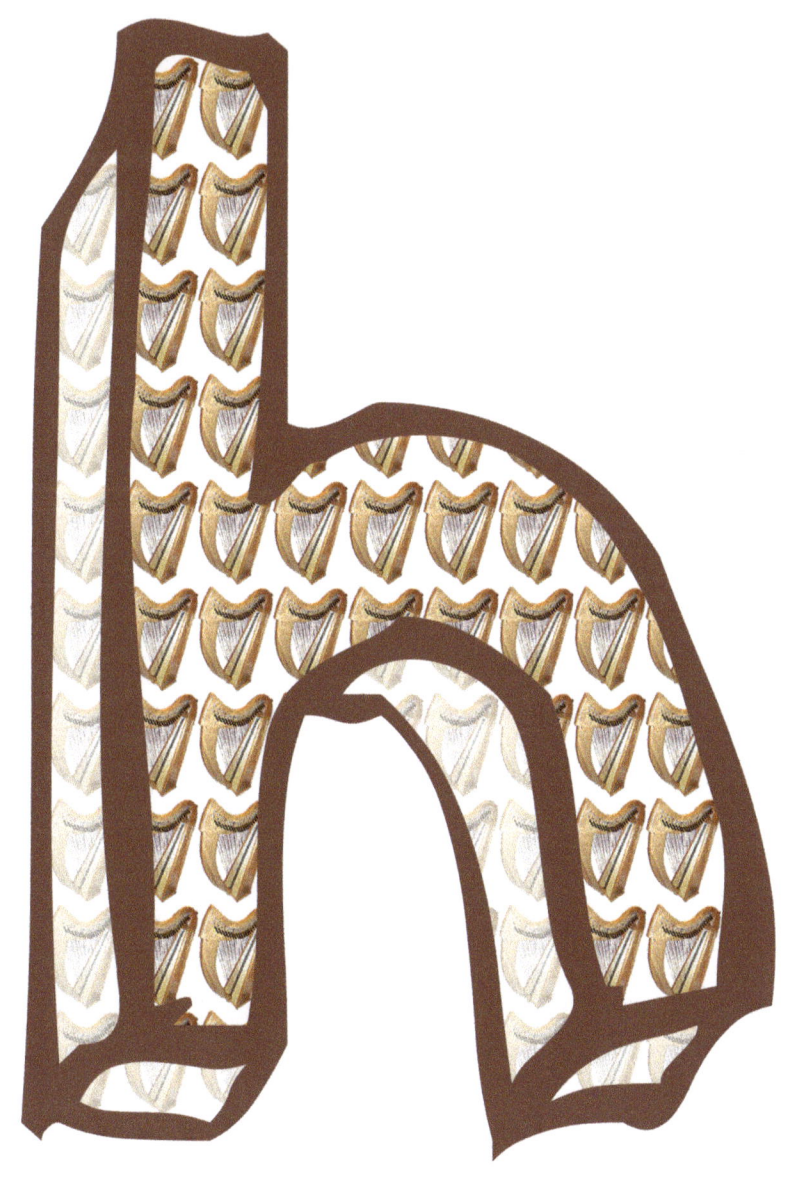

harp

Soft. Quiet.
Peaceful. Beautiful.

gumball

Stretchy. Chewy.
Bubbly. Sticky.

fish

Water. Swim. Splash. Flop.

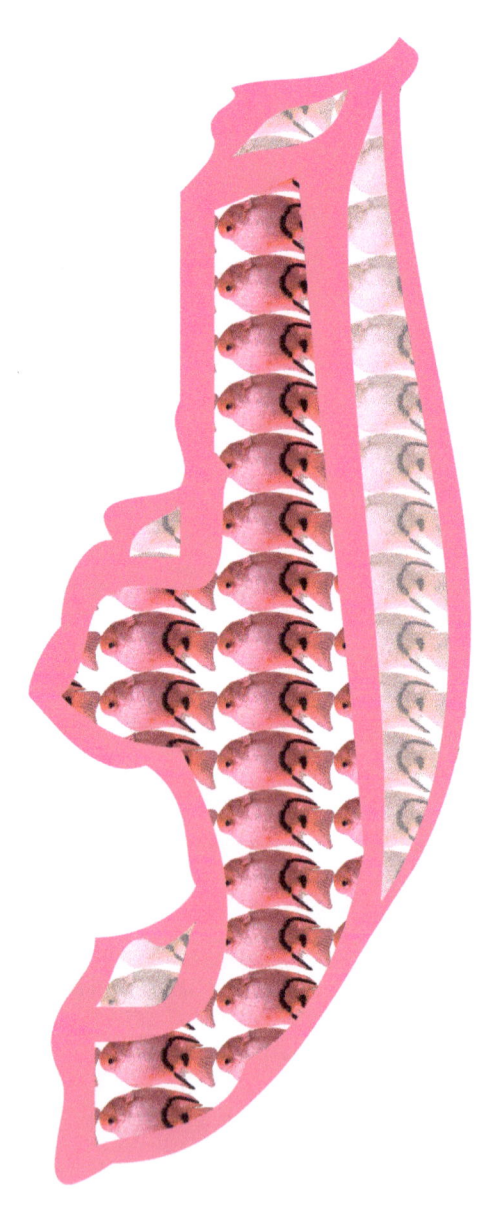

envelope

Address. Lick. Close. Stamp. Mail.

duck

Bird. Beak. Webbed feet.
Quack. Quack.

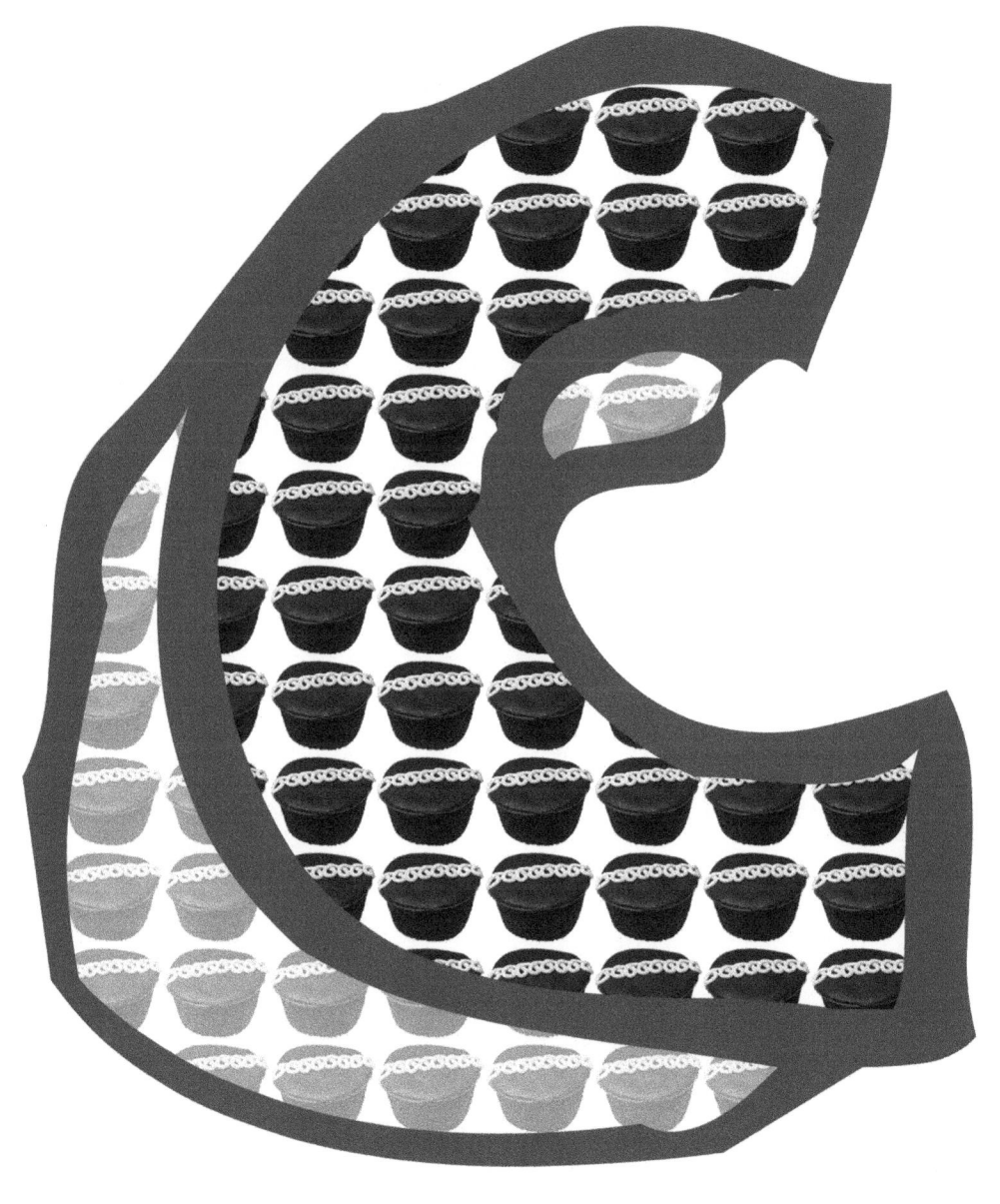

cupcake

Cake. Frosting.
Chocolate. Vanilla.

bicycle

Wheel. Handle. Spoke. Pedal. Ride.

apple

Round. Bite. Crunch. Sweet.

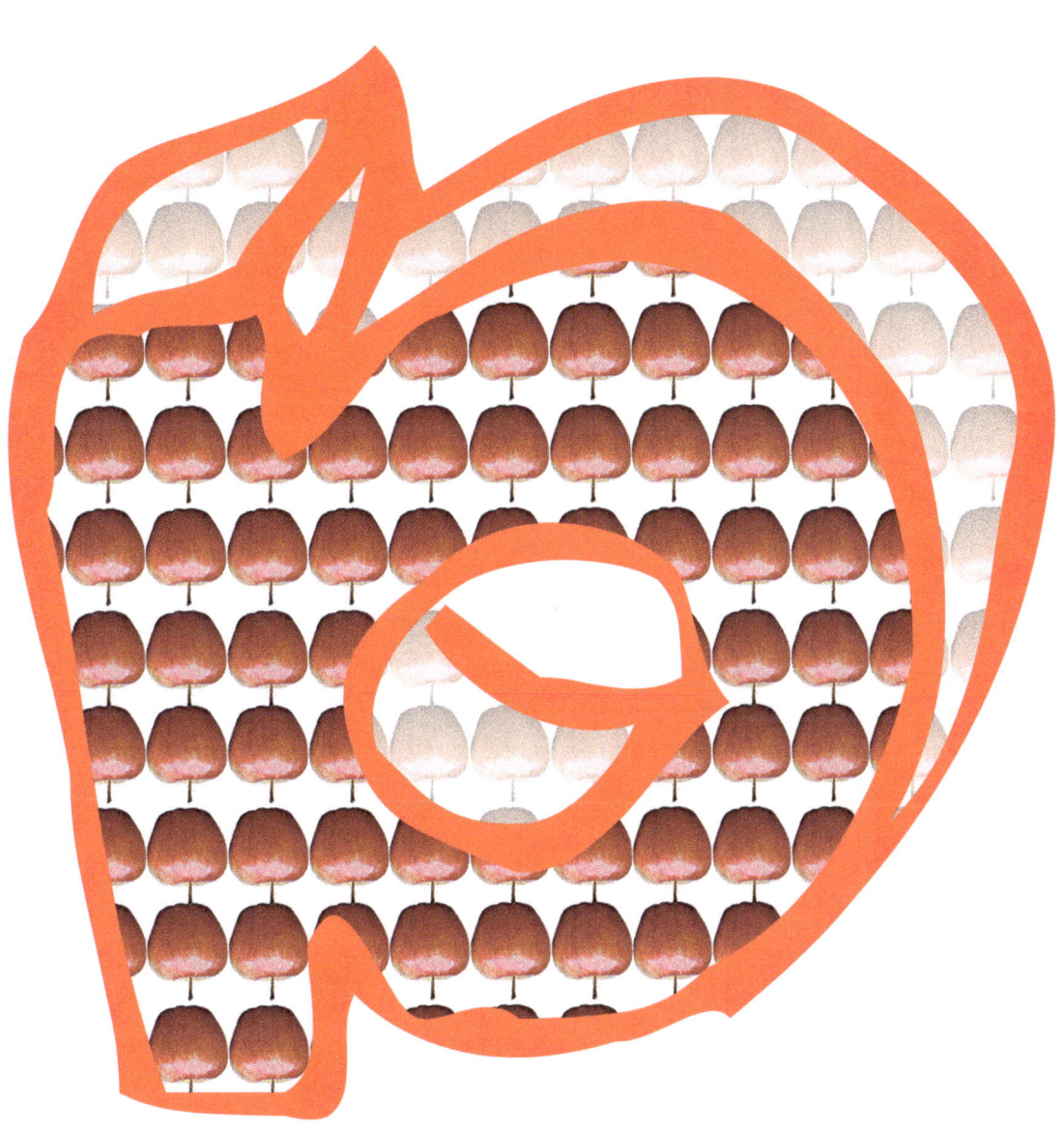

Copy. Print. Trace. Learn. Repeat.

abcdefghijklm

nopqrstuvwxyz

abcdefghijklm

nopqrstuvwxyz

abcdefghijklm

nopqrstuvwxyz

abcdefghijklm

nopqrstuvwxyz

www.ingramcontent.com/pod-product-compliance
Lightning Source LLC
Chambersburg PA
CBHW040731020526
44112CB00058B/2944